UNSTUCK

The Ultimate Guide to Getting and Staying Motivated

Dr. Shannon Simpson Shand

ALL RIGHTS RESERVED. No part of this book or its associated ancillary materials may be reproduced or transmitted in any form or by any means, electronic or mechanical, including photocopying, recording, or by any information storage or retrieval system without permission of publisher.

PUBLISHED BY:

SHANNON SIMPSON

DOUGLASVILLE, GA

DISCLAIMER AND/OR LEGAL NOTICES

While all attempts have been made to verify information provided in this book and its ancillary materials, neither the author nor publisher assumes responsibility for errors, inaccuracies, or omissions and is not responsible for any monetary loss in any matter. If advice concerning legal, financial, accounting, or related matters is needed, the services of a qualified professional should be sought. This book or its associated ancillary materials, including verbal and written training, is not intended for use as a source of legal, financial, or accounting advice. You should be aware of the various laws governing business transactions or other business practices in your state. The information contained in this book is strictly for educational purposes. Therefore, if you wish to apply ideas contained in this book, you are taking full responsibility for your actions. There is no guarantee or promise, expressed or implied, that you will earn any money using the strategies, concepts, techniques, exercises, and ideas in the book.

STANDARD EARNINGS AND INCOME DISCLAIMER

With respect to the reliability, accuracy, timeliness, usefulness, adequacy, completeness, and/or suitability of information provided in this book, SHANNON SIMPSON, its partners, associates, affiliates, consultants, and/or presenters make no warranties, guarantees, representations, or claims of any kind. Participants' results will vary depending on many factors. All claims or representations as to income earning are not considered as average earnings. All products and services are for educational and informational purposes only. Check with your accountant, attorney, or professional advisor before acting on this or any information. By continuing with reading this book, you agree that SHANNON SIMPSON is not responsible for the success or failure of your personal, business, or financial decisions relating to any information.

PRINTED IN THE UNITED STATES OF AMERICA | FIRST EDITION

© All Rights Reserved. Copyright 2023. SHANNON SIMPSON

Dr. Shannon Simpson Shand

CONTENTS

Introduction	5
13 Ways to Motivate Yourself	6
10 Ways to Stay Motivated for Working Out	9
7 Ways To Motivate Yourself To Do Things You Don't Want To Do	13
The 15 Commandments of Intrinsic Motivation	19
A Foolproof Formula for Staying Motivated During Online Learning	22
Understanding Inspiration	28
The Best Things You Can Do When You Feel Unmotivated	31
8 Ways to Inspire Yourself and Others	35
6 Reasons You Lose Motivation After Getting Started	38
11 Tips to Self-Motivate	41
Top 6 Reasons Why You Haven't Found Your Passion	44
10 Fast and Furious Ways to Get Out of a Rut	47
14 Ways To Rejuvenate Your Passions This Spring	50

UNSTUCK

Top 10 Inspirational Sayings	53
The Power of Motivating Imagery	56
How to Go from Stuck to Unstuck	59
Taking Action	61
Learn the Skill of Self-Motivation	63
Combating Mental Fatigue	66
Top 10 Tips for Staying Motivated When You're Unemployed	68
Skyrocket Your Success With a Motivating Morning Routine	71
Affirmation Reflections	**74**
Inspiration Journal	**85**
Conclusion	**116**

INTRODUCTION

Does it feel like people around you seem to have it figured out, achieving their goals, going places, having the best time of their lives, but you feel stuck and unable to get going? Are you at that point in your life where you feel overwhelming mental, emotional, or even physical paralysis? You are not alone. I know how it feels to be stuck in a rut. And I also know how to get out of the rut. That's why I am sharing this book with you.

My goal isn't to excite you with some momentary feel-good quotes. My desire is to open your eyes to the truth about who you are and guide you to how you can find purpose and joy. The truth is the answers you seek are already within you. You may not realize it yet, but you are more powerful than you think. Changing your life begins when you start changing your mindset. Perspective is everything!

It's time to break out from the confines of your own limitations and start permitting yourself to be free to live your best life. In this book, I share practical guides that can help you navigate life and reach your desired goals. Regardless of everything you have been through, you can go from where you are now to fulfilling your biggest dreams.

Let's get started!

13 WAYS TO MOTIVATE YOURSELF

Motivation never seems to last for long, but that's okay. There are so many ways you can rekindle your motivation. Begin each day by stoking your motivation. If your motivation wanes, you'll know how to give it a big boost.

Some people seem to be motivated all of the time. This isn't just a random phenomenon. They instinctively know how to motivate themselves. For the rest of us that aren't so lucky, we can learn.

Here are 13 strategies for you to use to give yourself a boost of motivation whenever needed…

1. Promise Yourself a Reward.

Give yourself something to look forward to! It could be something as simple as a magazine or elaborate as a trip to Thailand. Maybe you'll give yourself a quick TV break if you're able to get your household chores completed by a certain time.

2. Visualize Success.

See yourself being successful and experience how great it feels. If you expect to feel good about completing something, you'll be more likely to do it.

3. List The Advantages.

What are the advantages of getting your task completed? What benefits do you receive? Try using logic to your advantage. Remind yourself of what you're getting out of the deal.

4. List The Disadvantages.

Use pain to your advantage. What are the penalties of not getting your task done? How will you suffer? What are the negative consequences? You can gain a lot of motivation by recognizing the advantages and disadvantages of taking or not taking action.

5. Remind Yourself Of How Successful You've Been In The Past.

If you're lacking in motivation because you doubt yourself, remember how well you've done before. Give yourself a boost of confidence, and you'll feel more motivated.

6. Just Get Started, And The Motivation Will Come.

Sometimes you need to get to work and then the motivation will show up. Get started and see what happens!

7. Watch An Inspiring Video.

Avoid the temptation to waste too much time watching videos, but a short, inspirational video can help get you started.

8. Listen To An Inspiring Song.

Put on some music that inspires you and get things done!

9. Read Inspiring Quotes Or Books.

Again, avoid wasting too much time. A few inspirational quotes or maybe a chapter of an inspirational book will be enough to light your fire.

10. Declutter Your Work Area.

It can be hard to feel motivated when you're trying to work in a cluttered area. Spend a few minutes and tidy up. Avoid using this as an excuse to clean your whole house. You don't need to clean the refrigerator to get work done at your desk.

11. Focus On Just A Few Tasks Each Day.

Shorten your to-do list and you'll feel less overwhelmed. A feeling of being overwhelmed tends to decrease motivation and productivity.

12. Avoid Worrying About The Things That Don't Matter.

Keep your mind on the things that matter and you'll better preserve your motivation. There aren't that many things you need to do each day that are crucial.

13. Set Very Short-Term Goals.

Very short term can mean a week or 10 minutes. Whatever works for you is acceptable. See how much you can get done in the next 15 minutes. If you do this enough times each day, you'll be amazed at how much work you can get done.

Avoid worrying if your motivation seems to run low. There are many ways to regain your lost motivation. Motivation is temporary, that's why it's necessary to reestablish it on a regular basis. Motivation is the juice that allows us to get things accomplished. Knowing how to generate it at will is a powerful skill.

10 WAYS TO STAY MOTIVATED FOR WORKING OUT

When we get a new exercise regimen or diet program, we get excited and can›t wait to start exercising and eating right. But soon after that, we get bored and go back to our old habits.

This cycle is why it is important to stay determined, maintain motivation, and set goals for yourself.

What can you do to stay motivated? Try these tips...

1. Set some goals.

Begin with a few easy goals and work your way up. For example, you could start by walking instead of taking the bus or subway to work. You might decide to eat healthier and cut out specific unhealthy snacks.

- By setting attainable goals, you keep your motivation high.

2. Make it exciting.

Exercising doesn't have to be a chore. The best way to stay motivated is to keep your routine interesting. Try something new. Join a Zumba class or take up kickboxing. Doing something you genuinely enjoy can make a real difference.

- If you try to do too much at once, you'll likely end up discouraged – and your workouts will end up lacking.

3. Write it down.

What would you like to achieve: thinner waist, toned arms, more muscle? Write them down. You get motivated to follow your exercise routine when you visualize the results and write down your intentions.

- You can also keep an exercise journal. Make a record of what you do each session. Record your feelings after each workout. Putting down these pieces of information helps to keep you motivated.

4. Reward yourself.

Treat yourself to something nice after completing a workout. Even the most minor rewards can motivate you to work out. For example, reward yourself with a new pair of shoes when you achieve a longer-term goal.

5. Don't expect a miracle.

Avoid expecting immediate results. Don't be discouraged by how hard you workout. Commit to working out and eating nutritiously each day and you'll soon see results if you stick to your routine.

- Some people assume that they'll suddenly wake up one day and begin to enjoy working out and eating healthy. That's true to some extent. You'll find it easier to work out with time. But there will never be one big moment where you're suddenly ecstatic about working out.

6. Listen to a podcast that your friends are crazy about.

We all have specific interests, and some of us have a wide variety of desires. Some people like anime and manga, while others like hunting, fishing, and hiking; others like sports, dramas, comedies and the like.

- Find out what interests you and pair it with your exercise routine. This technique known as temptation building was created by an associate professor at the University of Pennsylvania. She discovered that students who restricted themselves to listening to audiobooks only at the gym had a 29% likelihood of working out more than those who could listen at any time.

7. Give yourself a good pep talk.

When you find that a particular workout is boring, give yourself a little pep talk. Talk about how you feel, what you're looking forward to, and why you should work hard.

- It will motivate you. Out of boredom, your workout routine can become tiresome. It's painful, and you might end up hating it. That's why getting a little pep talk can be very helpful.

8. Enjoy some good music.

Putting on some upbeat music while you work out can be a lot of fun. Music is an excellent way to boost your mood. It's also a great way to get out of a rut.

- When you listen to music you enjoy, you have a better chance of working out, because it gives you a positive attitude.

9. Spend some money on yourself and the routine.

Buy some new gym clothes or a gym membership. Doing these things show that you're dedicated, so you'll feel more motivated.

10. Leave the past behind you.

You may not have been the most athletic person in high school. Maybe your schoolmates used to laugh at you because of your physique. Leave the fears and scars of the past in the past and look forward to achieving your goals in the future.

- Your first thought may not be to get fit or stay in shape, but if your mindset is in the right place, these fears will vanish. Focus on the present. Think about your fitness goals rather than your past failures.
- This process will help you get motivated and put more effort into your workouts.

Staying motivated is hard, but you can do it. Listen to your favorite music before your workout. Remind yourself why you want to get in shape and visualize yourself and your life once you achieve those goals.

Doing these things shows that you're dedicated. Greater motivation always results from greater commitment. Get started today! You'll be glad you did!

7 WAYS TO MOTIVATE YOURSELF TO DO THINGS YOU DON'T WANT TO DO

It's likely that your biggest challenge isn't that you don't know what to do. It's the fact that you can't reliably get yourself to do what you know you should do.

If you could get yourself to do the hard things…you could successfully follow any diet, any exercise routine, stay away from your ex, keep your house clean, save money, or ask for that promotion. You'd never procrastinate.

We're all severely limited by the things we can't get ourselves to do. We know plenty, but we have poor self-management skills. It's hard to think of a skill that could impact your life more.

Use these strategies to change your life by getting more control over yourself…

1. Consider what you have to gain by taking the undesirable action. What are the advantages of getting this task done? What do you have to gain? Make a long list of advantages and use logic to your advantage.
2. Consider what you have to lose if you don't. Now, do the opposite. Imagine the worst that can happen if you fail to

act. Make a list of everything that could go wrong. What are the disadvantages of putting this task off? Make it painful to procrastinate.

3. Focus on how great you'll feel when it's finished. Visualize completing the task. Focus on how wonderful it feels. Imagine all the benefits you'll gain. Notice how happy you feel to finally have this monkey off your back. Now do the opposite. Vividly visualize not doing the task and experience all of the negative consequences. Make yourself feel as horrible as you can. Don't worry, it's in your best interest!

4. Release the tension. Imagine doing the tasks and notice where you feel tension in your body. Keep thinking about performing the task and relax those uncomfortable areas of your body. When you can think about the task and not experience a negative reaction, it will be much easier to perform that task.

5. Start very small. Sometimes, the best way to get yourself to start is to start small. It might be a single phone call, five minutes of work, or cleaning out one closet. Break your task down into bite-sized portions that you can handle with relative ease.

6. Promise yourself a reward. Bribe yourself. Perhaps it's a candy bar, dinner with a friend, or a new TV. Avoid putting yourself into debt, but desperate times call for desperate measures.

7. Get a friend to help. Give a friend an amount of money that's really meaningful to you. It might be $10 or $1,000. Now, tell your friend not to give it back to you until you've completed the task.

You can really turn up the heat on yourself by giving yourself a deadline. Tell your friend they can spend the money if you don't complete the task on time!

If you could get yourself to do everything you knew you should do, your life would be unrecognizable. You already know enough to have a much, much better life!

Information is hardly the problem these days. However, we still aren't any better at managing ourselves.

If you can master this one skill, everything is within your grasp. All you really need to do is learn how to get yourself to do the hard things. If you can do that, life is easy!

Gain Inspiration From the Success of Others and Soar to New Heights!

When you're feeling dejected for your inability to hit targets, it pays to seek outside inspiration. What better place to find inspiration than in the stories of successful people!

However, mere admiration of those people is inadequate. Your aim is to do what they do, so you can have the kind of success they've found. Once you've learned the formula, you'll realize you have what it takes to be great too!

Use these strategies to become inspired by the success of others:

1. **Interview successful people.** Successful people are all around you. They may be in your family, at your workplace, or in your community. Make an effort to sit with them and understand their inspirations. Take the time to transfer that knowledge to your plan of action.

    - What makes them tick? What gives them the drive to go after the next goal? You'll likely discover they find their own inspiration in whatever means the most to them.

    - Learn what you can about how the road to each goal was traveled. The ups and downs of life contribute to the pride you feel once you achieve a desired goal.

2. **Take a shot at similar goals.** Consider the kind of goals successful people set their sights on. Is there a common denominator? How does each goal relate to the others? Consider a similar path.

- Often, you'll find that each objective of someone successful ties into their overall mission in life. Perhaps their goal is gratification, in other cases it may be wealth or status.
- Consider whether their overall mission relates to yours. Then and only then can you proceed with going after similar goals. Otherwise, stick to what matters to you.

3. Showcase your skill set. Embrace your abilities and use them to go after specific goals. It›s possible that your current ambitions aren't the ones destined to bring you great success.

   - Believe that your strengths are meant to be used for greatness. It's certainly possible to acquire new skills. But avoid overlooking what you're naturally good at. Your talents may make achieving goals an even quicker process for you.
   - Find ways to use your natural abilities to help others in need. Sometimes profound success comes out of charity!

4. Sharpen weaker abilities. Those who are successful try to continuously get better. Just like you, they have weaknesses. But what›s important is the effort you make to overcome them. What are your weaker abilities?

   - Successful individuals learn something new every day. They use every opportunity they have to increase their knowledge base. As you continue to learn new skills and sharpen your current ones, you'll find more opportunities opening up for you.

Greatness is a state of mind. It can easily transform your life into a series of incredible successes. Just consider how it transformed the lives of those who shared their success stories.

UNSTUCK

You're just as talented as those who are successful, so it's a great idea to be inspired by them. But more importantly, recognize that their inspiration helps you identify how much talent you already have. You possess the ability to achieve any goal that's important to you!

THE 15 COMMANDMENTS OF INTRINSIC MOTIVATION

Intrinsic motivation can help you live better and accomplish more. Learn how to take more satisfaction in everything you do rather than depending solely on external motivators. These 15 commandments will help you to set your own course and live a fuller life.

Selecting Meaningful Activities

1. Identify flow experiences. You've probably heard about flow. Those are the occasions when you get so caught up in what you're doing that you lose track of time. You enter a blissful state where everything seems effortless.

2. Keep a feelings log. If you need help determining what conditions trigger flow for you, try starting a journal. You may find that gardening or number crunching gets you fully engaged. It may turn out that you're a morning person or that you do your best work after dinner.

3. Set specific goals. Learning and progressing are also essential to keeping an activity interesting. Give yourself measurable targets and timelines to aim for.

4. Take on new challenges. Stretch your abilities by venturing into new areas. Put yourself to the test with something that's demanding, but within reach. Rehearse a new piece of piano music or prepare to take a certification examination for a popular software program.
5. Streamline your schedule. On the other hand, you may also benefit by removing some tasks from your to-do list to make more time for things that are most important to you.

Making Every Activity More Meaningful

6. Understand the motivation continuum. Many experts believe that most of our actions reflect a combination of intrinsic and extrinsic motivations. For example, you may value both your paycheck and the contribution your job makes to society.
7. Participate more intensely. Sometimes a boring task can be transformed by turning it into a game. When cleaning out the garage, try to guess how long a can of paint has been there.
8. Adopt deep learning strategies. Choose study methods that help you to retain more knowledge. Think about how the facts relate to your own life. Evaluate what you read. Write down your own summary of the material you've covered.
9. Enlist support. Working in groups can liven up a tedious chore. Gather your neighbors together to spruce up a local park. Share responsibility whenever possible.
10. Clarify your purpose. Ask yourself why you're doing something. It's easier to exercise when you remember that you want to lose weight.

11. Radiate enthusiasm. A positive attitude will make any job less stressful. Smile and look on the bright side. For example, if you're dreading your grocery shopping, find a reason to laugh while doing it.

12. Exchange feedback. We can all help each other to feel motivated by being willing to share constructive feedback. Provide tactful and timely information on how to get better.

13. Seek variety. Alternating between tasks can help you stay fresh. Devote 15 minutes at a time to completing your expense reports and filing documents. You may find both projects more pleasant.

14. Get adequate rest. Building regular breaks into your schedule also keeps you motivated and in top condition. Make time for play and reflection. Stick to a consistent bedtime and take naps if you need to supplement your overnight sleep.

15. Serve others. All work becomes more joyful and fulfilling when you view it from the perspective of how it helps others. There are certain careers and activities that lend themselves to this. Maybe you do volunteer work at the local animal shelter. Or perhaps you are a nurse or a teacher that helps others on a daily basis. Assisting others is motivating!

Welcome more fun into your life by letting your passions drive you. Even washing the dishes will become more satisfying when you align your daily activities with internal sources of motivation.

A FOOLPROOF FORMULA FOR STAYING MOTIVATED DURING ONLINE LEARNING

How can you stay motivated when learning is online? In the classroom, you have a teacher to engage you in the subject and other students to socialize with. When it's just you and your laptop/tablet, etc., you'll need to take charge of your experience.

Fortunately, you have plenty of role models to learn from.

Even before the pandemic, more than 6 million students were enrolled in distance education and at least 77% of US corporations have incorporated it into their programs, according to the Online Learning Consortium.

Find a balance that will enable you to continue your education while fulfilling your other responsibilities. Try this formula for making learning effective and fun.

Staying Disciplined with Online Learning:

1. Set goals. Keep your purpose firmly in mind. Remember your main objectives, whether you want to finish a degree

you started years ago or increase your appreciation for art.

2. Plan your week. Block out time for your most important activities. Tackle demanding tasks during the hours when you're usually at peak performance.

3. Establish routines. Cutting down on daily decisions can make you more efficient. Adopt habits like doing your assigned readings one hour before bedtime.

4. Limit distractions. Focus your attention on your studies. Keep your phone and TV turned off during school hours.

5. Start small. Baby steps build momentum and make big projects seem less overwhelming. Break your work down into specific measurable tasks. You might spend a morning outlining your research paper or summarizing your notes.

6. Dress up. Putting on clothes that make you feel good will probably make you more productive. Keep yourself well-groomed even when you're alone and off camera.

7. Perform reviews. Work on your study skills. Ongoing reviews of your class materials will help you to remember what you've studied and may help you earn higher grades.

8. Take tests. Research shows that practice tests are one of the most effective ways to learn. Your teacher may provide them, or you can write your own.

9. Create priorities. Respect your limits. If you're adding coursework on top of your other responsibilities, give yourself adequate time for sleep and other essentials. Scratch some other items off your to do list if possible.

10.

Having Fun with Online Learning:

1. Connect with others. You can still enjoy a sense of community while studying online. Ask your teacher about their communication preferences so you can stay in touch and ask questions. Participate in student chat rooms and virtual study groups.

2. Decorate your space. Designate an area for your school activities with aesthetics and ergonomics in mind. Display your favorite photos or a green plant. Ensure that you can maintain correct posture while reading and typing.

3. Reward yourself. Give yourself incentives to excel. Maybe you'll want to order sushi for dinner each time you get an A. Maybe you'd like to spend an hour reading novels for each hour you spend solving math problems.

4. Play games. Make your assignments more entertaining. Challenge your classmates to some friendly competition. Invent funny sentences and songs that help you to memorize dates and names.

5. Take breaks. Building adequate downtime into each day will help you to reduce stress and achieve more. Take a ten-minute break each hour. Extend your lunch hour so you can go for a walk or lift weights.

6. Share support. Ask your family and friends for the help you need. If your kids are attending school online, do your homework together.

If your coworkers are signed up for the same course, stick around for a virtual happy hour or coffee date afterwards.

Earn a degree online or use your time at home to deepen your knowledge about any subject that interests you. Being able to motivate yourself will help you to persevere and succeed at online learning.

Extrinsic Versus Intrinsic Motivation

Extrinsic motivation is when you do something to receive a reward or to avoid punishment. For example, a child wants to make the basketball team so he/she can be popular and get closer to the cheerleaders.

Intrinsic motivation is when doing an activity is rewarding in and of itself. A child wants to be on the basketball team because he/she loves to play basketball. Or he/she's fascinated with the idea of learning the game. The reward is internal.

Consider these examples:

- Most people don't go to work because they love going to their job (intrinsic). They go because they receive money for it (extrinsic).
- A child does her/his chores because she/he wants to receive a reward or to avoid punishment. (extrinsic)
- Do you love the idea of starting a business because the challenge excites you (intrinsic)? Or, do you dislike the idea of starting a business, but the potential financial reward (extrinsic) is intriguing enough for you to do it?
- Do you truly enjoy spending time with your partner (intrinsic), or is the primary reward the financial security, companionship, and the opportunity to have children (extrinsic)?
- Do you stay with your partner for love (intrinsic), or because the consequences of leaving would be too difficult (extrinsic)?

- Do you struggle to accomplish anything without deadlines (extrinsic)? Or, do you love the feeling of getting your work done and can't stop yourself from doing it as soon as possible (intrinsic)?

We all have intrinsic and extrinsic motivators.

Because intrinsic motivation relies directly on how you honestly feel about something, this type of motivation is a more effective way of creating long-term happiness.

If you want to develop more intrinsic motivation in your day-to-day life, these techniques will help:

1. Make a list of the things you love to do. If your doctor tells you that you need more exercise, there are many different types of exercise you can do. You could play tennis, run, swim, lift weights, or play soccer. If one of those activities is very enjoyable to you, it only makes sense to choose that activity.

    - Whenever you need to do something, consider the most enjoyable way to accomplish it. When you can find something you enjoy, it will be hard to stop yourself from doing it.

2. Learn how to reward yourself. A reward can be as simple as pumping your fist in the air and congratulating yourself. Avoid using an external reward system if possible.

    - Imagine that you want to do 25 pushups each morning. After completing your pushups, you jump up in the air and tell yourself how awesome you are. In time, that simple reward can make pushups enjoyable and attractive. This is also how habits can be created.

3. Understand WHY you are doing something. Even the smallest of tasks can be linked to a greater purpose. Playing

piano scales might seem mundane, but if you believe they are an integral part of learning to master the piano, they seem a lot more meaningful.

Most people can't fathom why a millionaire or billionaire would continue to work. That's because most people work only to make money. Take the money away and they'd quickly stop going to work. Give them enough money that they don't need any more, and they'll quit.

However, the billionaire becomes a billionaire because he loves building and creating. His main motivation is intrinsic. The money is secondary. That's why he never stops working.

Intrinsic motivation will keep you coming back for more. Extrinsic motivation is less reliable. When the external reward vanishes or becomes less enticing, you'll stop repeating that behavior.

Find things you love to do, and then do them. Use your natural interests to your advantage and greater happiness will be the result.

UNDERSTANDING INSPIRATION

Inspiration is a curious thing. It's been described as exalted and divine. It's also part of ordinary life. It's something that comes to you without any effort on your part. It's also something that you can influence with your actions.

Dictionaries define inspiration as a kind of sudden mental stimulation. A brilliant idea pops into your head while you're taking a shower. Something you see out a car window triggers thoughts for a new invention or a different career.

Learn more about how inspiration can brighten your life, along with strategies for enjoying more aha moments.

Benefits of Inspiration:

1. Change your behavior. Research shows that adults who experience higher amounts of inspiration tend to have more compelling goals and make more progress in realizing them. It's another reason to keep challenging yourself.

2. Increase your engagement. Inspiration transforms your to do list from things you have to do into things you want to do. Your life has more purpose.

3. Enjoy greater happiness. Imagine being excited about Mondays and doing laundry. Inspiration wakes you up to the beauty of daily life.

How to Feel More Inspired:

1. Build your self-esteem. Researchers have also examined personality traits associated with inspiration. A healthy self-image is essential. Accept and appreciate yourself for who you are.

2. Think positive. Optimism helps too. Look on the bright side and focus on the things you can control. Take a break from TV news if it's making you feel anxious.

3. Cultivate gratitude. Being thankful is especially powerful. Keep a journal to remind you of your blessings. Let others know that they make a difference in your life.

4. Be spontaneous. When was the last time you did something on the spur of the moment? Shake up your routines by packing a picnic lunch or building a fort with your kids.

5. Honor your needs. You're more likely to feel transported when you work at staying fit. Eat a nutritious diet, exercise regularly, and aim for 7 to 8 hours of sleep each night. Manage stress and take refreshing breaks before you feel fatigued.

6. Observe role models. Enthusiasm is contagious. Surround yourself with friends and colleagues who feel passionate about what they do.

7. Continue learning. Devote yourself to lifelong education. Read books and listen to podcasts about a wide range of subjects. Keep adding to your knowledge and skills.

8. Try new things. Exploring unfamiliar territory helps you to overcome fears and think more flexibly. Substitute an exercise class for your usual bike ride. Volunteer at a local food bank or animal shelter.

9. Make art. Block out time each day for creative activities. Work on your hobbies or start a new craft project. Visit art supply stores and read magazines for ideas.

10. Practice patience. Dramatic flashes and profound insights can be few and far between. Remember that gradual developments can also pave the way to success.

11. Take action. On the other hand, you may sometimes speed up the process by taking a first step while you're waiting for inspiration to strike. If you're low on energy, pick up a paint brush or work in your garden for 10 minutes. You may find that you've built up enough momentum to want to continue.

12. Limit competition. While there are many sources of inspiration in life, comparing yourself to others may backfire. Some studies show that less competitive personalities experience more inspiration. Enjoy your work and learn from experience, instead of worrying about impressing others.

Open up more possibilities in your life. Being inspired will help you to accomplish great things and have more fun along the way.

THE BEST THINGS YOU CAN DO WHEN YOU FEEL UNMOTIVATED

We know that self-motivation is vital for work. There's a good chance we can keep going despite trials with high motivation levels. But life gets in the way.

Unexpected events cross us every day. And depending on how we react to them, these events can throw us off balance.

It's even more so now that many people find themselves working from home. With zero self-motivation, you may become frustrated, unproductive, and ineffective.

Fortunately, there are things you can do to avoid this. For example, you can schedule your daily work tasks according to your calendar. Additionally, you can manage your day. If you wake up late, don't start your day with Twitter.

Instead, you can make the most of every waking moment.

Try these tips to increase your motivation:

1. Set goals. A big reason for feelings of demotivation comes from not knowing where we want to go. Why do you wake up each morning and go to work? What would you like your

life to look like in the next year or two? Why do you want your life to look that way?

- Asking these questions helps you gain a clear objective about where you want to head. Once you have answers to these questions, you can finally set the goals that are right for you.

2. Avoid comparing yourself to others. People know they are imperfect by nature. But they forget this when they compare themselves to others, thinking they have to perform better than everyone else. This action leads to more stress and depression.

    - Instead of comparing yourself to others, try imagining what your life will be like when you achieve your goals. This approach can help you eliminate the endless lists and mental comparisons that hinder your progress.

3. Wade through your struggles. Everyone has challenges in their lives, so it's easy to have negative thoughts and emotions. Instead of abandoning your goals, try to face your problems and figure out what you can do.

    - Your challenge may feel like a huge obstacle, but giving up on your dreams is a much bigger deal.

    - Remember why you started. Recognize that results don›t come instantly. Stay motivated and keep looking toward your goal.

4. Let your choices differ from the past. Everyone hates change. But many times, that's what we need. You don't have to make significant changes to your life. Instead, you can make small changes that lead to substantial results.

- For example, someone trying to lose weight might choose to eat healthier and exercise more. Someone trying to stop smoking may think about trying a different alternative. Someone interested in starting a business may look for free ways to market their product.
- Your results will follow your decisions, so choose wisely!

5. Embrace your mistakes. We all make mistakes. Even if you're doing something right, sometimes you will still make an error. Learn from your mistakes and move on. Realize that mistakes are as natural to humans as breathing.

    - Even the most successful people have made poor decisions at one time or another. And the truth is, mistakes help us to grow as we learn. They allow us to learn new skills and improve our behaviors.
    - So instead of dwelling on your mistakes, evaluate them and think about what you did well. By doing this, you will learn from your mistakes and achievements, making you more motivated in the long run!

It's easy to feel unmotivated. However, the key to staying motivated is to focus on the big picture.

While it's true that you may never reach some goals, if you focus on the possibilities and work hard to meet them, you can still achieve your dreams no matter how difficult they may be.

Rewards encourage consistency.

I treat others with the same kindness that I extend to myself. It is important for maintaining trust in relationships. I celebrate my achievements as well as those of others.

Although I sometimes set different standards for myself than for others, I extend rewards based on outlined expectations.

Knowing that there is a system of rewards encourages me to be consistent with my actions. This approach works with maintaining a lifestyle of wellness. Complying with daily fitness goals is easy because I acknowledge my own positive results.

I treat myself to a spa day when I hit a major milestone on my fitness journey. It is important to keep myself motivated for the long term.

The same approach works with my kids and their chores. Instead of requiring occasional conformance, I challenge them to make doing chores a part of their norm. I treat them to their favorite dessert after a week of good work.

When doing performance evaluations of my staff at work, I celebrate small things. When they see that even small efforts are rewarded, I gain their commitment to bigger ones. Sometimes starting small produces lasting and meaningful results.

Today, I use a formula of rewards to encourage ongoing positive behavior. I am happy to highlight any person's achievement when doing so encourages them to keep up the effort.

Self-Reflection Questions:

1. What are some of the rewards that I extend to my colleagues at work?
2. How do I ensure that I continue to be a committed friend?
3. What actions am I consistent with without receiving rewards?
4.

8 WAYS TO INSPIRE YOURSELF AND OTHERS

Inspiration is everywhere, although it's not always as easy to spot during challenging times.

It can be easy to get stuck in a rut and, once you get there, it can be difficult to get out. But you can find inspiration for yourself and others all around you.

It's important to remember that inspiration means different things to different people. What someone finds stimulating, someone else may find little value or beauty in. If you're going to find your own flash of creativity, you can look for what you're interested in.

What to Look for When Inspiring Others

Since you may not always know what others like, it can be difficult to get through to others and inspire them. Rather than showing others what inspires you - which might not work for them - strive to teach others how to look for the spark they seek. When they know what to look for, they'll be able to see inspiration every place they look for it. Consider:

1. Breaking down a larger object into fine details and study those details carefully.

2. Analyzing a conversation for subtle nuances that might give you ideas to work with.
3. Looking more closely at something you generally only see from a far-away distance.
4. Using a writing or drawing prompt to get your creative thoughts flowing more easily.
5. Thinking, looking, or listening outside of the box to see new ideas and opinions.
6. Asking others about what inspires them and looking for the hidden beauty in those things.
7. Taking a class in something you've never done before or a language you want to learn.
8. Traveling to a place you've never been to see the culture and beauty there.

When you teach someone how to locate ideas on their own, they'll possess that skill all their life. Then they can find their own excitement wherever they are: at work, home, or on the go. It's a simple strategy that's great for the creative type, or for anyone who feels stuck in a rut.

Open Your Eyes to Inspiration

Inspiration seems to come more easily to some people than it does to others. Because of that, some people can quickly find stimulation while others remain in a pattern of thinking that tells them strong positive emotions are out of their grasp.

Finding that creative spark is within your reach, if only you'll make the conscious decision to leave your comfort zone in favor of new experiences. Be willing to make mistakes, look silly sometimes, and live life to the fullest. Creative inspiration is as close as your next decision to try something new.

When you step out of your comfort zone, you'll be different from the crowd, but you'll live a life filled with colors, textures, and a richness that many miss. Decide today to try something out of the ordinary, and see what creativity flows from you and to you when you do. You deserve all that life has to offer. Why not make a new choice today?

6 REASONS YOU LOSE MOTIVATION AFTER GETTING STARTED

Have you ever made big plans for your life, only to fail to act on them? Or maybe you started with a bang and kept your motivation for a few days, but suddenly lost interest.

It's easy to lose motivation after the initial excitement wears off. But if you want to be successful, it's important to keep going. The work isn't going to get done itself.

Understand why you lose your motivation:

1. **The planning phase is more fun than the execution phase.** Sitting alone at night and making plans for the future can be an exciting time. Everything seems possible because you're only limited by your imagination at that point.

   - However, when the sun comes up in the morning, it's time to actually get busy. It all seems a little more daunting and less enjoyable when it's time for the rubber to hit the road.

2. **You lose track of the end result.** Remind yourself of the prize at the end of your journey. Visualize how it's all going to be when you've reached your goal. You should feel an immediate boost of motivation.

3. Your goal doesn't suit you. Many of us choose goals that are acceptable to the world at large. It might be buying a huge house or a fancy car. Maybe your goal is totally mismatched to your real desires or temperament. Ensure that you've chosen goals that match your interests and abilities.

4. You feel uncomfortable and aren't dealing with it effectively. Of course, it's uncomfortable to do anything new. Whether it's creating a new income stream, beginning a workout routine, or a new diet, it's going to be uncomfortable. It's important to deal with this discomfort effectively.

    - Expect to feel uncomfortable. Have a plan for working through it. If you're making changes to your life, discomfort is the norm.

5. You have too many negative thoughts. Negative thoughts are paralyzing. Negative thoughts will make you rationalize that you should quit. Though it doesn't always feel like you have control over your thoughts, you do. You can choose what you want to think about.

    - Take control of your thoughts. Catch yourself early in the process of thinking negative thoughts and redirect your focus to something more positive. It takes time to develop this ability. The key is to notice quickly that your thoughts are going off the rails.

6. You're stuck in your old habits and routines. The older you are, the more challenging it can be to break out of your old patterns. We find comfort in our old routines, and our brains become hardwired to repeat them. You'll need to create new habits and routines if you want to change your behavior or your results.

- Identify one habit that is getting in your way and one habit you need to create to attain your goals. Put your time and energy into dealing with these two items. When you're successful, tackle two more.

Which of these six reasons applies to you most often? Is there another reason you fail to sustain your motivation? Motivation and willpower can be highly variable.

Expect that your motivation will falter and be prepared to deal with it. Focus on creating habits that will take you to your goals, because habits reduce the need for motivation and willpower.

11 TIPS TO SELF-MOTIVATE

Even the most experienced and successful achievers can use a little help getting motivated from time to time. Motivating yourself is a learnable skill. Everyone procrastinates; it's human nature. Several tactics and strategies can lift your motivation to the critical level necessary to get yourself moving again.

Try these techniques to motivate yourself and get things done:

1. Choose happiness. It's much easier to motivate yourself when you're in a positive mood. Focus on the wonderful things in your life that fill you with gratitude. When you do, cleaning out the garage won't seem quite as daunting. Keep your mind on the positive things in your life.

2. Learn how to be a finisher. A trail of unfinished projects can dampen anyone's enthusiasm to start another. Avoid quitting before a task is 100% completed. You'll be more interested in taking on new tasks when you expect to be successful. Success breeds success.

3. Expect mistakes. The only people that don't make mistakes are those who never do anything. The more mistakes you make, the more you'll learn. Mistakes can be very positive. Use them to your advantage.

4. Keep yourself grounded in the present. If you're worrying about the future or beating yourself up over the past, it's challenging to get anything accomplished right now. Focus on your breathing for a few minutes if your mind is running wild.

5. Focus on the result. You'll find it difficult to get started if you sit around and think about all the work that needs to be done. Focus on the result and you'll feel more motivated.

6. Give yourself a reward. You go to work every day because you know that a paycheck is coming your way. You wouldn't go otherwise. Give yourself a small, but meaningful, reward when your work is complete. Determine the reward before you get started.

7. Use a timer. Decide how long a task should take and see if you're right. Set a timer and see if you can beat the clock. A little time pressure will help to keep you focused on your work. There are many timer apps and programs available at no cost.

8. Read inspirational quotes. Reading inspirational quotes by those who have achieved great success can be very motivating. Spend a few minutes reading these great quotes and you'll be sure to experience an enhanced level of enthusiasm. Consider creating a list of quotes that you can keep nearby in case of an emergency.

9. Consider the price of failure. What is the price of failing to follow through? Make a list of the negatives. Some of us are more driven by pain than we are by reward. Using both to your advantage can be powerful.

10. Get some exercise. If you're feeling stuck, go for a brisk walk or a short run. Taking a short break every 60 minutes has been shown to increase productivity. Keep your breaks short so you don't get off track.

11. Measure your progress. Big goals or projects can take years to complete. Measuring your progress along the way is a great way to keep your spirits high. Set short-term goals to keep you focused.

Most of us don't live with our mothers any longer. It's important to be able to motivate ourselves. The most successful people are able to harness the power of self-motivation. A higher level of motivation will ensure that your work is done well and as quickly as possible. It's time to get busy!

TOP 6 REASONS WHY YOU HAVEN'T FOUND YOUR PASSION

Are you living your life passionately? Life is too short to be slogging along without a sense of passion and purpose in your life. However, that's exactly the way most of us live our lives. What happened to the exciting and ambitious ideas you had as a child? Are they gone forever?

You're going to have to work diligently at whatever you choose to do if you want to be successful. It only makes sense to spend that time and effort on something that's meaningful to you. Can you be more committed to your freedom and happiness than you are to your comfort zone?

Find your passion and experience life to the fullest!

Are these reasons keeping you from discovering your passion?

1. You lack the necessary experience. While a few people choose the course of their lives by the age of six, most of us need more experience to make that determination. You can't know what it's like to play the piano, race a car, or write a screenplay until you've actually spent some time doing those things.

- Passion comes from experience. Spend some time doing the things you think you might love to do.

2. You're too comfortable and have forgotten what you love. Dreams and passion start to die as soon as you take a job primarily for financial stability. You quickly lose sight of what you love to do in the name of comfort and convenience.

    - Spend some time thinking about and experiencing the things you once loved to do. It might spark some new ideas.
    - Avoid being too practical. You're more capable than you believe. Nearly any passion can be turned into a significant income.

3. Your ideas lack a creative component. People are destined to create something. Whether it's molding the minds of children in the classroom, designing a skyscraper, or owning a string of dry cleaners, many careers thrive with creativity. No one fantasizes about working in a cubicle.

    - In most cases, your greatest passions and utmost joy will come from something that allows you to be creative.

4. You're projecting too far into the future. It's easy to become discouraged if your passion will take a long period of time to achieve. Becoming a rock star or an orthopedic surgeon won't happen overnight. It's easy to think that all the steps leading up to a big goal are meaningless.

    - But all of those steps are part of the journey and just as worthwhile. In fact, they're not just obstacles, but learning opportunities necessary to make your passion a reality.

5. You're unclear about your values. When your values are crystal clear, it's much easier to make decisions and plot your course.

What's most important to you? Create a list of your values. You'll find that this exercise is highly useful. It will help to define you as a person.

6. You're not good at dealing with discomfort. When you think about your passion, you might feel uncomfortable. After all, if you're sleeping on your mom's couch with $37 dollars to your name, how will you ever become the world's most powerful sports agent? You must be able to step out of your comfort zone in order to change your life for the better.

No matter how you've been living, you can change. The difference between pursuing your passion and taking the safe boring path is tremendous. Regardless of your age, you can begin living your passion right now. You give your best to the world and your family when you're excited, committed, and fully engaged.

10 FAST AND FURIOUS WAYS TO GET OUT OF A RUT

We all get stuck in ruts from time to time. You know you're in a rut when every day seems the same, and those days aren't very enjoyable. After a while, it's hard to know the best way to bring about the changes that can make life exciting, interesting, and enjoyable again. Ruts tend to be self-perpetuating and require a decent amount of energy to get back out.

Implement these 10 strategies to get out of your rut:

1. Realize that your discomfort is a good sign. As humans, we tend to feel uncomfortable when we experience a change in our lives. Accept the fact you might have some challenging feelings to navigate as you come out of your rut and get your life back on track.

2. Find a passion or interest to add to your life. Now's the perfect time to take up yoga or the guitar. If you've always wanted to learn how to paint or try out mountaineering, go for it!

Your concerns and worries vanish when you're involved with something that fascinates you.

3. Make a list of the things you've never tried, but have always wanted to. Find one or two things that interest you the most and give them a shot.
4. Schedule your new activity. Make your new hobby a priority by scheduling it into your life. It should get the high-priority status it deserves.
5. Look for a new job. Work takes up a lot of our waking hours, so life is much more enjoyable when you like the field you choose. If you feel like you're in a rut, maybe a career change is in order. There's no reason to spend the majority of your adult life in a career that doesn't interest and excite you.
6. Get physical. Sometimes we spend so much of the day sitting and staring at a computer screen that we forget about our bodies.
    - A body can't stay healthy if it doesn't get the chance to stretch, move around, and exert itself a bit each day.
    - If you're not active, consider adding some exercise activities to your day.
7. See the doctor. If multiple aspects of your life seem to be in a rut, it might be time to see the doctor. It's possible that an underlying health issue might be the culprit of your rut.
8. Start small. It can be overwhelming to change every aspect of your life at once. Avoid trying to change too much too quickly.
    - Make a list of everything you would like to change about your life.
    - Start with either the easiest or most meaningful change.
    - Plan the best course of action for you at this time. You can

always add additional changes over time.

9. Set a goal. If you're lost, sometimes a goal is the best tool to refocus. Having a clear target can help you stay on track.

    - A goal provides a clear, measurable, and time-based objective.
    - The key is to pick a goal that will enhance your life.

10. Go someplace new. Have you ever noticed you have a different perspective when you're in an airplane and look down? Life just seems a little different.

    - Experience a new location. The different surroundings and people are bound to alter your outlook on life. You might only have to hop in your car and head for the city or mountains.

Jumpstart your life today and get out of that rut. Remember you'll have to adjust your behavior if you want your life to change. Give these tips a fair chance and you'll be pleasantly surprised with the results. You can start small but start today.

14 WAYS TO REJUVENATE YOUR PASSIONS THIS SPRING

Spring gives the perfect opportunity to shake off your winter doldrums! Get in tune with all the new growth around you and make some positive changes in your life: try these 14 ways to rejuvenate your passions.

Rejuvenating Passions in Your Professional Life

1. Reconnect with former colleagues. If you're feeling more energetic now that the days are getting longer, use that time to look up people you've fallen out of touch with. Strengthen your network. Call up an old coworker to get together for lunch.

2. Learn a new skill. Ask your human resources department about any training programs available in your workplace. Order a catalog from your local community college. Take a course on project management or negotiation skills.

3. Brighten your office. Hang up new wall art or change your computer wallpaper to a new image like colorful birds or a country setting. Pick up a pretty desk lamp at a thrift shop.

4. Switch to a standing desk. Improve your health and boost

your energy levels. Stand up while you work. Studies show that you may add an average of three years to your life.

5. Edit your resume. Give your resume the once over. Add in your most recent accomplishments. You'll feel more motivated and better prepared for your next job search or performance evaluation.

6. Be kind to your coworkers. Helping others is the most effective path to happiness. Offer praise generously. Pitch in when you see a coworker struggling with their workload.

Rejuvenating Passions in Your Personal Life

7. Volunteer. Share your high spirits with others that need it in your community. Spend a weekend afternoon sorting cans at a neighborhood food bank. Register for a walkathon for your favorite cause.

8. Exercise outdoors. Take a break from the treadmill. Join a softball league or play volleyball on the beach. Browse online for outdoor tai chi or yoga classes.

9. Update your look. When you look better, you feel better. Treat yourself to a spa day. If money is tight, give yourself some home treatments like a rose water skin toner or avocado hair conditioner.

10. Tend to your garden. Gardening is good for your body and mind. Mow the lawn and prune trees and shrubs that may have been damaged over the winter. Get ready for your pretty new flower beds.

11. Banish clutter. Give yourself more breathing room. Use spring cleaning as an opportunity to discard things you rarely use. List them for sale online or donate them to a charity shop.

12. Go on a double date. See your partner in a new light by going out to dinner with another couple. You'll have fun and discover new ways of interacting. If you're between relationships, organize a group activity where you can meet new people with less pressure than on a conventional date.

13. Unleash your creativity. Make time for creative pursuits. Visit an art museum and really engage with the works. Tour an art supply store for new ideas for craft time with your kids. Build a birdhouse out of wood or from a gourd you grew yourself.

14. Indulge in spring vegetables and fruit. Seasonal produce is one of the greatest pleasures of spring. Whip up a parfait of mixed berries, granola, and yogurt. Try sauteing asparagus in garlic and butter.

As the temperatures get milder and flowers pop up everywhere, feel your hopes soar. The spring season is the perfect time to welcome more passion into every aspect of your life.

TOP 10 INSPIRATIONAL SAYINGS

We all have those moments when we need inspiration to gain confidence and build momentum. That's why inspirational sayings are so popular!

When you live a life without inspiration, it can be a life without any real joy or passion. In those moments where you need a little pick me up or a reminder of the many great things you have in your life, you can turn to the power of inspirational words. You need to have a collection of inspirational sayings in your toolkit that resonate with you so you can get more done and still feel great!

The Top 10 Ten Inspirational Sayings You Can Use Everywhere!

There are a lot of great motivational sayings out there that we can turn to when we are feeling down, but we should be using them all the time, rain or shine! Strive to incorporate inspirational sayings into your everyday life, by using them to inspire you to reach higher and push harder to achieve all of the things you have set out to do and more.

Some wonderful inspirational sayings include:

1. There is a beautiful light at the end of my tunnel.
2. I take small steps in life and value my time.
3. In order to share happiness with others, I must also be happy.

4. As I let go of dissatisfaction, I feel happiness in my life.
5. My life is full of purpose, exciting change, and many recognized deeds.
6. No matter the challenge, I will see it through.
7. I am becoming more focused and confident every day.
8. I welcome positive energy and I use that feeling to accomplish more.
9. My life is already full of success.
10. I keep only two mental snapshots of myself: where I am and where I want to be in life.

These are all very simple inspirational sayings that work to affirm positive thoughts and attitudes in your mind. Affirmations are simply positive statements that remind you of your goals and positive uniqueness so you can boost your self-confidence.

Accomplish More with the Power of Inspirational Thinking

Inspirational sayings and affirmations can help us move forward in life and accomplish greater things than we could have ever imagined. After all, we can't deny the power of a can-do attitude. If more of us incorporate inspiration into our lives, we would all be happier and more successful people. When you incorporate positive sayings into your life, you'll find that you'll respond on a subconscious level and you'll no longer need to look very far for inspiration!

If you're down or lacking confidence, you can use inspirational sayings to find the courage to move forward and force out any negative thoughts that may be cycling through your mind. When you say these statements with gusto, you are re-affirming positive thoughts in your mind, making them a part of who you are.

Remember to use these sayings at any and every occasion to give you the inspiration you need to get through any challenge, both big and small.

THE POWER OF MOTIVATING IMAGERY

Do you suddenly feel a surge of energy when you look at a picture of your children? Do you ever see a picture and remember that is why you are working so hard every day?

The power of motivating imagery is immense and can work for you in your everyday life no matter what your struggles are. The right image can help you get through almost anything.

Using Motivating Imagery Wherever You Go

Where do you turn when you're at home and you need a bit of motivation? You may have pictures of your family or perhaps pictures from a previous vacation. You can look at those to remind yourself why you do what you do.

It usually isn›t difficult to find motivation when you're at home because you're in the midst of all that you've worked hard to accomplish. But what happens when you're at work and dreading every minute of it?

When you're at work and your boss has just finished his annoying rant, or your co-worker just finished disturbing your peace, you need a quick source of motivation to keep pushing forward. Where can you find that burst of energy when you're in the middle of a busy workday?

- You don't have to look any further than your computer for all the motivating imagery you need.

Escape From Stress With Motivating Computer Wallpaper Backgrounds

You can download motivational wallpapers to your computer desktop so that when you're in the middle of those stressful moments, you have a source at your fingertips to inspire and motivate you.

These inspirational images can serve as a powerful reminder of why you work so hard. If nothing else, you can lose yourself in the image for just a moment. This can help ground you and let you see the world in a different light.

- A moment of refreshment recharges you and gives you the power to attack your to-do lists in a positive and systematic way.

There are many types of inspirational wallpapers for you to choose from. Many of them are simply inspirational images, while others combine a quote or affirmation with a scenic picture. These can be very powerful because they use images and words, the two things that the mind responds to the best.

When you're having a hard time, you can look at the picture and escape from the whirlwind that surrounds you. As you do this, you'll begin to feel peace return to your life in a matter of a few seconds.

Motivating imagery can work wonders. Whether you're sitting in your office or away on business, you may just need something calming, familiar, and reassuring to bring back your motivation and inner peace.

UNSTUCK

The great thing about the wallpapers is that they don't take up any space, they're often free, and no one has to know they're there. You can use these images whenever you're at your computer and need a helping hand. This is a quick and easy tool that has the power to recharge your batteries during a tough day.

HOW TO GO FROM STUCK TO UNSTUCK

If you find yourself stuck, perhaps it's time to explore the reasons why. With some simple self-exploration, you can pinpoint the areas of your life that require change. It may require you to leave your comfort zone, but in the end, you'll likely find that it was all worth it!

It's also important for you to build an action plan. If you stay organized and follow a simple plan of action step by step, there will be nothing that can stop you from achieving your goals.

Here are some ideas that can get you on your way to getting unstuck:

1. Set Up Accountability. When you hold yourself accountable and keep a close eye on your goals, you'll be better able to identify when you're stuck in a rut. The first step is to really figure out why you're feeling stuck in the first place.

2. Set A Time Goal. You're stuck and you'd like to be unstuck, but chances are you've been putting off working toward your goal. You've already decided to make yourself accountable and now it's time to give yourself a time limit - so do it!

UNSTUCK

3. Be Not Afraid. Being afraid of change is one of the biggest reasons why you get stuck in the first place. Perhaps you're feeling trapped in your job and, in order to get the job you'd like, you have to go back to college. You need to get over your fear and see what you need to do to apply. You'll be happy you did when you land your dream job someday.

4. Look For Role Models. Find someone who has been through your situation or something similar and see how he or she was able to overcome obstacles. If possible, ask this person questions.

5. Change Your Thinking. It's true: your actions first start as thoughts. You'll be motivated into action when you think positive and brave thoughts!

6. Take Time. Remember to take some time for yourself to collect your thoughts. You may discover some insight into how to solve your challenges. Make sure you're completely alone with your thoughts without any distractions.

7.

TAKING ACTION

It's easy to remain in your "stuck" situation because it's familiar and you know what's going to happen. You might even feel safe. However, eventually, the dissatisfaction you feel will take over and you'll realize that the only way to get "unstuck" is to take immediate action to change.

Make the Change

Once you choose your timetable, you'll want to break down your changes into small steps. Track your progress and tweak your system to make sure your changes are making a difference.

For example, if you're feeling stuck in a relationship, you'll first evaluate where you think the concern lies. Perhaps you aren't communicating effectively. If so, you can set a timetable of three months to overcome this challenge.

You can then break down the problem into smaller steps by reading a book on communication, talking about it with your partner, or attempting counseling sessions. As you go through these actions, you're constantly keeping a close eye on how it affects your relationship.

In the end, you'll have a firm decision about your relationship's progress and will no longer feel stuck. If you take no action, it'd be impossible to improve!

UNSTUCK

Repeat the Process

Once you've applied this system to one aspect of your life, you can use the same strategies whenever you're feeling stuck. Whether large or small, there are always actions you can take to break through barriers!

LEARN THE SKILL OF SELF-MOTIVATION

The ability to motivate yourself is necessary if you want to be successful. Everyone struggles to be productive from time to time, but there are several tactics that make it easier to get back on track. A few tips and new habits might be all you need to enhance your results dramatically.

Children have the benefit of parents, coaches, and teachers. As adults, we have to learn to manage ourselves. Unfortunately, few of us are taught this skill. We must learn on our own. Take solace in the fact that your peers are in the same situation. Plus, just think of how much ahead of them you'll be when you learn the art of self-motivation!

Use these techniques to motivate yourself and take control of your life:

1. **Use pleasure to your advantage.** Make a long list of the benefits of taking action. What will you gain? A better body? Improved social life? More money? Self-respect? When you find your motivation lagging, return to this list and rekindle your enthusiasm.

2. Use pain to your advantage. If you fail to act, what is the likely outcome? You'll be forced to live another day in your current existence. Or maybe your financial situation will become a little bit worse. Perhaps your income taxes will be late. Give yourself a list of painful outcomes to avoid.

3. Reinforce your lists daily. Read over your lists of positives and negatives each day. Keep them fresh in your mind.

4. Take a walk. A change of environment can help to clear your head and increase your level of motivation. It's a great time to think big thoughts and to consider long-term goals.

5. Create habits that support your goals. Ideally, you can structure your life so you don't require motivation. Are you motivated to take a shower or brush your teeth? Not really – you just do them out of habit. Creating habits that make your goals an automatic reality is the best motivation tool of all!

6. Ask yourself why you're stuck. Are you afraid? Tired? Restless? Figure out what's stopping you from taking aggressive action and getting things accomplished. Then take action to resolve the reasons for your inaction.

7. Make a plan for the day. Before you retire for the evening, make a list of everything you'd like to get done. Most importantly, get started on your list of items early in the day. Build momentum and the rest of the day will go more smoothly. Success builds on success.

8. Get started. Have you ever noticed that motivation happens after you get busy? It's interesting how challenging it can be to get started, but how easy it can be to continue. Pull

out every trick in the book to make yourself begin. The resistance you feel will decrease markedly.

9. Reward yourself regularly. Rewarded behaviors are more likely to reoccur in the future. Give yourself little rewards on a regular basis. You deserve it.

10. Compete with yourself. Strive to create small improvements in yourself each week. This can be more motivating than competing against others. There might be plenty of people ahead of you, but you can always do better than you did last week.

11. Eliminate distractions. Everyone has a preferred method of distraction. It could be the internet, television, or ice cream. Avoid allowing yourself to indulge in your distraction until you've accomplished something worthwhile. Be strong.

When you're feeling unmotivated, avoid the belief that you're stuck. There's always something you can do to lift your spirits and tackle those big projects. Develop the skill to motivate yourself. You can't be certain which tactics will be successful until you get started.

COMBATING MENTAL FATIGUE

Mental fatigue can take its toll on a person's well-being. It can be worse than physical fatigue because of a person's inability to think clearly or express their feelings and frustrations. Worse still, mental stress is known to cause physical fatigue and illness, too!

Mental fatigue or exhaustion may be a result of your work, family life, conflict, or even a lack of quality sleep. If you must make an important decision, mental stress can take its toll on you and can even lead to severe depression. This is even more reason to avoid the consequences and implement strategies to overcome mental fatigue!

How to Relax your Mind and Boost your Energy

Relaxation is necessary to relieve mental stress and rejuvenate your body and mind. You're probably thinking, "How am I going to do that?" Well, it's easy. Here are some tips to help you reduce mental exhaustion and start implementing a relaxation routine:

- Take time out for yourself. Spend time in a quiet room where you can reflect and get in touch with your spiritual side. Everyone has a different way of self-reflection. Some pray or meditate, others write in a journal or diary, while others simply allow their thoughts to gently release into the darkness and quietness of the room.

- Get plenty of sleep. Mental fatigue can exist no matter how much sleep you get, but sleep does help refresh your body and mind. Getting adequate sleep will eliminate a lot of your day-to-day stress. After all, the body will have a chance to repair itself and recharge.

- Free your mind from the problems that swirl around you. Take your mind off of those things that are causing you stress by working on a puzzle or spending time with friends and family. Or perhaps you need to go out for a nice dinner or weekend getaway to free your mind.

- Exercise regularly. Exercise causes your brain to release endorphins, which are known to make you feel happy. It's like the body's natural "high." Even if all you can do is take a 15-minute walk, take it. That can be great alone time for you.

- Try breathing exercises. When things get rough, take deep breaths in through your nose, hold it for 10 seconds, then release. You'll notice that this will relieve tension.

- Take a day in which you can do things by yourself. Take yourself out to a movie, go to a museum or art gallery, or do something you've always wanted to do but never made time for. In doing so, you'll be able to enjoy the peace and quiet of being alone.

Implementing Your Own Strategies

These are just some of the strategies to combat mental fatigue. You may have some other methods that help you relax and find peace in your life. Once you begin integrating these simple exercises into your day, you will begin to feel the weight lifted off your shoulders and before you know it, you'll feel like a brand-new person!

TOP 10 TIPS FOR STAYING MOTIVATED WHEN YOU'RE UNEMPLOYED

Losing your job is painful. There are many days when you may feel discouraged because the job market is complicated and the competition for jobs is fierce. In order to get through a period of unemployment, it's important to use whatever resources you can to stay motivated.

Try these tips to boost your motivation while you search for a new job:

1. Utilize the power of the internet. Save time and money! Many tasks that will help you get a job are activities you can do more efficiently online.

    - Research companies, fill out applications, and join online networking groups to streamline your job search.

2. Work on your job search each day. Spend five days of the week actively looking for a job. Pick the ones that will work best for you. In most cases, that would be Monday through Friday. Take the other two days off.

3. Use your unemployment funds wisely. Pay bills that are necessary but limit other things, like social outings, to a minimum.

    - If you need to borrow money from a friend or family member, do so. Having the money you need to get by will take a lot of stress off of you.

4. Eat nutritious food. Stressful times tend to weaken your immune system, so include plenty of extra fruits and vegetables in your diet to help your body be at its best. Protein is also necessary for keeping your energy levels up when you're looking for work.

    - Trying to gain or lose weight at this time doesn't usually work well. You're more likely to be successful with your weight goals if you put off dieting until after you've found another position.

5. Exercise regularly. Enjoy whatever type of exercise that you're used to doing. This can be dancing, running, walking, or any other type of activity that you wish.

    - Exercise reduces stress, gives you energy, keeps you alert, increases your feelings of well-being, and strengthens your health. All of these benefits will help keep you motivated while looking for a job.

6. Get plenty of rest. It may be difficult to sleep at times when you're looking for work, but it's better to try. For optimum benefits, shoot for 7 or 8 hours of good quality sleep.

    - Avoid caffeine or computer screens for several hours before bedtime to make it easier to get your rest.

7. Use your friends for support. Don't be afraid to enlist the help of your friends. Explain to them that you're between

jobs and actively looking for work. Tell them what you're looking for and your background and skills.

- Your friends may know of a company that is looking for someone just like you!

8. Make an effort to keep in touch with previous co-workers. Co-workers from your previous job may also have job ideas and leads for you.

9. Watch your transportation costs. Cutting back on your gas mileage will save you money. It will also prevent a lot of wasted time. Only go to companies that you've contacted and have an interview with, so you aren't just pounding the pavement.

10. Schedule some "me time" each day. When you're unemployed, you might find that you're actually working harder than ever. Plus, the stress is highly taxing – both mentally and physically. It's important to re-energize and boost your morale by engaging in activities that bring you pleasure.

- Try to spend an hour each day doing something you love. Whether you immerse yourself in a hobby or a good book, or even just take a nap, enjoy your special time however you like. Pamper yourself. You deserve it!

Finding a new job almost always takes longer than we want it to, but you can stay motivated by using these tips. Stay focused and dedicated, and your determination will pay off.

SKYROCKET YOUR SUCCESS WITH A MOTIVATING MORNING ROUTINE

Have you ever noticed if you have a good Monday, the rest of your week seems to work out pretty well, regardless of whatever else happens? It's also true that getting your morning off to a good start practically guarantees you'll have a good day.

A good morning routine takes a little effort to develop, but it pays off handsomely. A morning routine can give you that great start, every day, like clockwork.

Keep these tips in mind when creating your morning routine:

1. Get up early. Most people lie in bed until the last possible second. When they do get up, there's only enough time to get ready and barely make it to work on time.

    - You'll have to experiment personally with the proper time to get up, but you should be able to get up and get through your routine with time to spare.

2. A drink of water should be the number one thing on your list. After 7+ hours without any fluids, your body is craving water. Drink a big glass of water each morning and see how much better you feel.

3. Get some exercise in before work. Whether it's 20 minutes on the treadmill, a walk around the block, or some calisthenics, do something to get your blood moving.

    - This will keep you from being groggy at work, you'll likely lose a little weight, and you'll feel great.

4. Schedule a little quiet time. It's great to have a few minutes to meditate, go over your goals, or just relax. This time allows you to eliminate that anxiety or sense or rush that many people have every morning. You might want to use this time to read or work on a crossword puzzle.

5. Have a good breakfast. Start the day out right with a healthy meal. Momentum holds true here, too. If you start the day by eating well, you're more likely to make healthy food choices throughout the day.

    - Many health experts promote the idea that a good breakfast is key to getting yourself healthier and in better shape.

6. Go over your schedule for the day. Think about what has to be done. This will give you a good mental picture of what your day will look like.

    - Do you have any meetings? Are there any clients coming into the office? Are there any employee issues that need to be handled?
    - Instead of showing up at work and trying to figure out what's going on, go into work with a good handle on things.

7. Make it a habit. It takes about 30 days to form a new habit. Be diligent for the next 30 days, including weekends! Studies

have shown habits practiced daily are easier to form than habits that are on a variable schedule. Practice the same morning routine every day!

Developing a morning routine can really change your life. Your morning routine should be unique to you. With a little experimentation, you'll quickly discover the best morning routine for you.

You might think this seems like a lot to do each morning. It might be more than you're used to doing, but that doesn't mean it's too much.

There is no rule that states you must stay up as late as possible to get the minimum amount of required sleep and barely make it to work on time. You're free to shift a couple of hours from the evening to the morning.

By the end of the day, you're beat anyway. Most people accomplish very little after 9:00 pm. Go to bed early and get up early. You'll get a great jump on the day before anyone else even gets out of bed! And your new morning routine will be a perfect start to many great days ahead.

AFFIRMATION REFLECTIONS

Read affirmations out loud and repeat as many times as needed.

_____

_____

_____

_____

Each morning when I open my eyes, I acknowledge that I have been given another opportunity to do my best, so I commit to giving 100% effort to make the most of this gift.

I give my all in everything I do. I feel that if something is worth doing, then it is worth doing well. Even boring tasks command my best effort. I try to do them as quickly as possible to get them out of the way and move on to something more exhilarating, but I still ensure that they are done to the best of my ability.

Stressful, uncomfortable or difficult situations also tempt me to give less or give up, but I push past them and keep giving the most I can. As an employee, I recognize that I have this job because my employer needs me. I use that thought to remind myself of my responsibility to give all my effort to my daily tasks.

My relationships with friends and family also deserve my full effort to keep them positive and healthy. To strengthen our relationship, I keep in touch, uplift them when they need help, and take time to make cherished memories together. Today, I feel accomplished when I achieve good things because I know they come from my giving 100%.

Self-Reflection Questions:

1. Do I sometimes feel discouraged when my efforts aren't recognized?
2. Am I comfortable giving 100% even when it is unpopular with my co-workers?
3. Am I a good example for others to follow?

UNSTUCK

Each moment inspires me

There are many things in my world that can inspire me. I need only look around me to gain inspiration to change my life for the better.

I listen to my favorite music to become inspired. I listen to music that makes me happy and I am filled with inspiration to choose - and live in - happiness and joy. I am grateful for music. Music transforms my reality immediately.

I am inspired by nature. I enjoy watching trees transform and I am inspired by the seasons changing. Animals also inspire me. I love to see puppies roll around and be thrilled with their toy. Hearing them bark with glee makes me smile. They simply amuse me.

I am inspired by people. I encourage you to take the time to listen to their stories. It is amazing at how resilient we can be when we want to be. People watching is also a great past time when at the airport or gathering place. We can learn a lot from each other.

I am inspired by smells. Isn't it true certain perfumes can remind you of special people and amazing experiences? Marketing experts have proven, smelling popcorn popping at the movie theaters makes you want to buy it. The smell of the ocean can trigger those memories that transformed your childhood or vacation. My present reality pulls from those smells still and they make me happy.

I am inspired by books. I love to read, whether it is for pure enjoyment or learning more about the world and how things work. It has been proven that reading and those who read are more successful and better critical thinkers. Reading allows you to see life from different circumstances and vantage points.

I am grateful that I have eyes to see the beauty around me, ears to hear beautiful music, and a nose that remembers scents that develop into wonderful memories. I am happy that my taste buds work so that I can explore other cultures. Having an open and inclusive mindset can help you appreciate the different people around you.

Today, I feel blessed. I have a fully functional body that can enjoy and appreciate life. I am inspired to be more thankful for my blessed life.

Self-Reflection Questions:

1. What can I do to show more appreciation for life?
2. How can I show more appreciation to others?
3. What can I do to inspire others?

_____
_____
_____
_____
_____
_____

I've learned to motivate myself

The strongest incentives come from within. I think positive. I create empowering beliefs. I take responsibility for my decisions. My self-talk is kind and encouraging.

I learn from experience. I am comfortable taking sensible risks because I focus on what I must gain. I can use any circumstances to teach myself how to enhance my performance.

I create a starting point. I break big projects down into manageable tasks. Each victory inspires me to keep moving forward.

I turn my work into a game. I enjoy household chores and office paperwork when I adopt a playful attitude.

I listen to music. A lively soundtrack helps me to work harder without feeling pressured.

I take a break. I give my mind and body the rest they need to stay strong and resilient. I go outdoors to connect with nature. I sip a cup of tea to clear my mind and recharge my energy levels.

I establish priorities. I focus my time and efforts on projects that are meaningful to me. I scratch nonessential tasks off of my to-do list.

I remember my purpose. I meditate on the reasons behind my actions. I engage at work because I want to help others and support my family. I eat nutritious foods because I want a long and active life.

Today, I pursue my goals with enthusiasm and determination. I am driven to succeed. Now, how can my experience help you to be open to learn and master motivating yourself? I want you to focus on these self-reflection questions below.

Self-Reflection Questions:

1. What is one challenge I want to tackle today?
2. Why is gratitude motivating?
3. How does believing in myself help me to overcome obstacles?

I've learned to motivate myself

I am driven to succeed by my answers to the self-reflection questions. The good news, you have what you need to motivate yourself also.

I remember my purpose. Thinking about the reasons behind my activities makes me want to push myself. Housework and jogging are more appealing when I focus on taking care of my loved ones and my health.

I turn my work into a game. I have fun competing with myself and practicing my skills. I make up stories about what I am doing and I find ways to introduce more variety into my workday.

I boost my energy level daily. I take a walk around the block or do a few pushups to add a touch of variety and power. I play upbeat music and sing out loud to add joy. I enjoy a few deep breaths or share a laugh with a friend because loving and taking care of myself matters to me.

I give myself a pep talk. I review my past achievements and I recognize my progress. I remember to congratulate myself for making an effort and for my wins. I reassure myself when I run into obstacles or feel like I have lost at something. I treat myself with compassion and accept ups and downs as a natural part of life.

I take breaks. I give myself time to rest and recharge. I let go of matters that hold back my progress and I allow myself to see things with new eyes. A new perspective is sometimes all we need to change to welcome a win.

I collaborate with others. My motivation grows even stronger when I surround myself with others who share my passions. It's amazing how much farther we can go when we exercise in groups. Group activities reassure us that our efforts are not only important for us, but for others that depend on us. Feeling appreciated and needed is one of the greatest motivational factors in life.

I set goals that are exciting and realistic for me. I go after what I want. I take one step forward and I feel the need to follow through. I find something I can accomplish immediately, and I build momentum that carries me forward. We build the same way we walk, one step at a time.

I think positively. I tell myself that I can do this. You need to believe you can do it, so you are not the reason you quit when things are challenging. Anything worth having takes work and imagination. Innovation is a sophisticated word for believing with imagination. You have to be willing to think positively and go outside the box to innovate.

Today, I am eager to seize opportunities and persevere until I succeed. My motivation comes from within.

Self-Reflection Questions:

1. What can I do when my motivation starts to sink?
2. How does my diet affect my motivation?
3. How does gratitude help me to stay motivated?

Passion gives me energy.

I am filled with enthusiasm that gives energy to my passion.

With my energy, I think positively. I am cheerful and upbeat. I look on the bright side. I laugh and smile. I cultivate gratitude and pay attention to the happy events that happen each day.

I focus on the present moment. I do one thing at a time. I take deep breaths and make deliberate choices instead of drifting through life.

I block out time for activities that are important and meaningful to me. I spend time with my loved ones. I do meaningful work. I fill my leisure hours with enriching hobbies. I practice my faith.

I immerse myself in new experiences. Breaking out of my familiar routines livens up my day. I gain a fresh perspective. I see more possibilities.

I surround myself with family and friends who give me encouragement and support. My confidence grows. I feel capable of taking on greater challenges.

I express my creativity. I awaken my imagination. I generate new ideas.

I engage my curiosity. I ask questions. I take pleasure in learning. I follow my interests and change my environment. I read, take courses, and travel.

I find joy in giving. I use my strengths to help others. I share my time and talents. I support worthy causes and give back to my community.

Today, I am excited about life. I listen to my heart. I am happy and productive.

UNSTUCK

Self-Reflection Questions:

1. How can I tell if I am following my own passions or someone else's expectations?

2. What are the advantages of having more than one passion?

3. What would I do if I had an extra hour each day to spend on something I love?

_____

_____

_____

_____

_____

_____

_____

_____

_____

_____

_____

_____

Passion propels me forward.

Passion drives me to make progress. Aligning my actions with my passion gives me more energy. I feel enthusiastic about everything that I do. I become more deeply committed. I am resilient in the face of challenges.

Feeling fulfilled is the greatest reward that I receive from living a passionate life. My happiness and contentment come from sources that are more stable than money or praise. I learn and gain insights. I develop a sense of accomplishment. I take satisfaction in serving others.

I focus on activities that give me a sense of flow. I lose myself in what I do. Everything seems more effortless when I become fully involved.

My passion moves me forward with emotional connections. I open my heart and view others with compassion. I reach out to people and give them my undivided attention. I put myself in their position and express my gratitude for their kindness.

When my spirits are low, I look beyond my emotions and use my powers of reason to reignite my passion. I appreciate both the process and the outcomes. Preparing nutritious food helps me to stay healthy. I also enjoy the textures, aromas, and tastes of fresh vegetables and whole grains.

UNSTUCK

Today, I tap into my passion and devote myself to meaningful activities that make my dreams a reality.

Self-Reflection Questions:

1. What kinds of situations spark my creativity?
2. What are three new activities I want to try?
3. Why is it important for me to recognize that passion exists inside of me rather than seeking it from external sources?

INSPIRATION JOURNAL

Your work can be exhilarating when you're filled with enthusiasm and purpose. On the other hand, even your favorite activities may require more effort on the days when you're feeling uninspired.

Finding inspiration and making it last helps you to unleash your creativity and reach your goals. Fortunately, those sparks are all around you when you're open to seeing them.

You can find inspiration anywhere you look:
- Playing with your children
- Volunteering at a senior center
- Making up a story
- Going sailing
- Watching a cartoon
- Drinking a cup of tea
- Growing orchids

Inspiration takes hold when you're passionate about achieving something and confident that you can do it. These simple daily exercises will help you to feel more motivated and take action.

UNSTUCK

Spending just a few minutes a day going through the prompts in this journal can make a big difference. You'll figure out what's holding you back and open up new possibilities.

How can you make your workplace more inspiring?

How can you serve as an inspiration to others?

UNSTUCK

How can you benefit from knowing how to inspire yourself?

Inspiration also means inhaling. How does your breath and posture help you to feel motivated?

UNSTUCK

How does nature inspire you?

Describe a time when you had an unexpected brainstorm. What led up to that experience?

UNSTUCK

Who are 3 historical or literary figures that you would choose as role models? What is it about their lives that moves you?

How does your environment affect your creativity?

UNSTUCK

How can taking action lead to inspiration?

Varying your routine can help you to feel more inspired. List 5 changes you can make this month.

How would you describe an inspirational leader? What kinds of qualities do they possess?

What are some unusual sources of inspiration that you have discovered?

UNSTUCK

Art can be inspiring. Visit a museum or browse around online to find interesting images. What is it about them that you find stimulating?

How does taking care of your physical health help you to feel more enthusiastic?

How does working out and moving around help to sharpen your thinking?

Imagine that you've been asked to give an inspirational speech to your local community. What would your message be?

UNSTUCK

What can you do to sustain inspiration for the long term?

Great ideas can come to you when you're taking a shower or doing other routine tasks. Has this ever happened to you? What great ideas have surprised you?

UNSTUCK

Travel can change your thinking. Pick a destination and describe why it would be illuminating.

How do you feel when you're inspired?

UNSTUCK

What kinds of books and movies stimulate your imagination?

What time of day do you feel most creative? How is this time different?

UNSTUCK

How can you savor moments of inspiration?

What is one creative thing you can do each morning?

UNSTUCK

What is the relationship between inspiration and intuition?

How can meditation give you new insights? Try it and see!

UNSTUCK

Are there any areas in your life where you feel stuck because you're waiting for inspiration? What are some different approaches you could try?

How can you share your feelings of inspiration online and offline?

UNSTUCK

What does it mean to inspire by example? How can you do this?

How can you motivate yourself to work when you're feeling uninspired?

___
___
___
___
___
___
___
___
___
___
___
___
___
___
___
___

CONCLUSION

People like to talk about how happy they want to be in life and how purpose is the ultimate thing they want. The first step to happiness is knowing that you are enough, and you deserve to be happy. Happiness doesn't happen by wishing for it, neither does it come by coincidence; it is making deliberate efforts towards being happy. It is embracing your imperfections while striving to become better. Seeking is good, but the biggest validations about who you are should come from you. So, wake up each morning and decide to choose happiness and hope.

Pursue purpose because it is the reason for your existence. It is the reason you wake up in the morning. If you have yet to realize your purpose, it is never too late to discover and nurture it. It is intricately connected to how happy you will become.

Set measurable goals and aspire to become something greater than yourself. Be inspired by other people's success. However, don't let it make you feel any less of yourself. Remember, the only person you are trying to outdo is YOU, not anyone else.

The most fulfilled people in life are not those who have everything. Rather, they are those who celebrate every little victory and win they have. You don't have to wait until you achieve the biggest dreams before you are happy. Be content with the little wins and each milestone.

Life may have dealt you some hard blows but dare to believe again! Aim for the future of your dreams and work towards their realization. All that you need for life and greatness are already embedded in you. Don't allow yourself to remain stuck.

In place of regret, fear, and self-criticism, allow joy, hope, and your self-esteem to blossom. Negative feelings will only keep you stuck; don't feed them. As you go through the different phases of life, maintain a positive attitude.

Finally, memorizing and rehashing motivational books and quotes will have no real impact on your life unless you back them up with actions and a solid plan. When you take everything, you read in this book and apply it in your daily life, you will go from being uncertain of who you are to making vital decisions that positively affect your life and that of other people around you.

An avalanche of unique potential is trapped within you, but will you leave your comfort zone and reach for them today?

www.ingramcontent.com/pod-product-compliance
Lightning Source LLC
Chambersburg PA
CBHW052108110526
44592CB00013B/1523